Just Voices
Showtunes

Published by
Novello Publishing Limited
14-15 Berners Street, London, W1T 3LJ, UK.

Exclusive distributors:
Music Sales Limited
Distribution Centre, Newmarket Road,
Bury St Edmunds, Suffolk, IP33 3YB, UK.

Music Sales Pty Limited
20 Resolution Drive, Caringbah, NSW 2229, Australia.

Order No. NOV940786
ISBN: 978-1-84772-689-6
This book © Copyright 2008 Novello & Company Limited.

Edited by Rachel Payne.
Music processed by Paul Ewers Music Design.

Printed in the EU.

www.musicsales.com

Just Voices
Showtunes

NOVELLO PUBLISHING LIMITED
part of The Music Sales Group
London / New York / Paris / Sydney / Copenhagen / Berlin / Madrid / Tokyo

Close Every Door

(from ''Joseph And The Amazing Technicolor® Dreamcoat')

MUSIC BY ANDREW LLOYD WEBBER – LYRICS BY TIM RICE

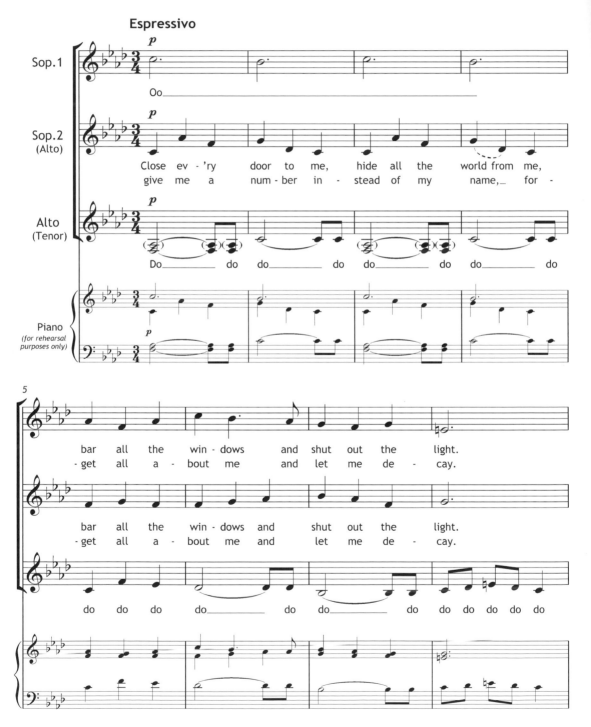

Oo_____

Do what you want with me, hate me and laugh at me,
I do not matter, I'm only one person, des-

etc.

dark-en my day-time and tor-ture my night.) If my
-troy me com-plete-ly, then throw me a-way.) If my

cresc.

If my

7

life were im - por-tant I would ask will I live or die, but

life were im - por-tant I would ask will I live or die, but

life were im - por-tant I would ask will I live or die, but

I know the ans - wers lie far from this world.

I know the ans - wers lie far from this world.

I know the ans - wers lie far from this world. _____

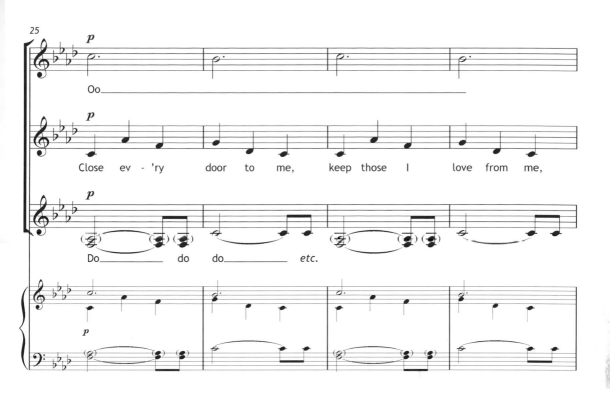

Oo_____

Close ev - 'ry door to me, keep those I love from me,

Do_____ do do_____ etc.

child - ren of Is - rael are nev - er a - lone. { For I / For we

child - ren of Is - rael are nev - er a - lone. { For I / For we

{ For I / For we

9

know I shall find my___ own peace of mind, for
know we shall find our___ own peace of mind, for

know I shall find my own peace of mind, for
know we shall find our own peace of mind, for

know I shall find my own peace of mind, for
know we shall find our own peace of mind, for

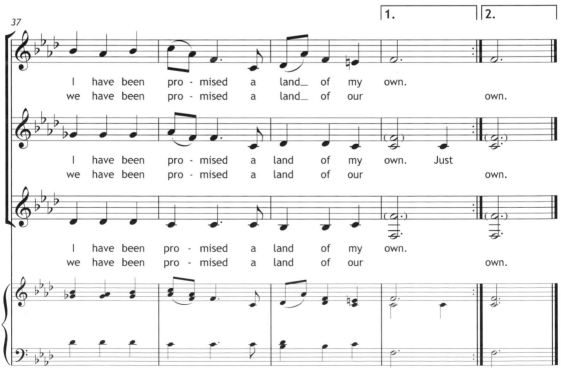

1.   2.

I have been pro - mised a land___ of my own.
we have been pro - mised a land___ of our   own.

I have been pro - mised a land of my own. Just
we have been pro - mised a land of our   own.

I have been pro - mised a land of my own.
we have been pro - mised a land of our   own.

The Rhythm Of Life

(from 'Sweet Charity')

WORDS BY DOROTHY FIELDS – MUSIC BY CY COLEMAN

Moderately

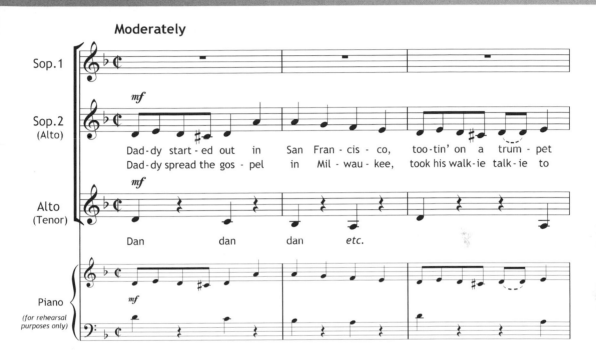

Sop. 1

Sop. 2
(Alto)

Dad - dy start - ed out in San Fran - cis - co, too - tin' on a trum - pet
Dad - dy spread the gos - pel in Mil - wau - kee, took his walk - ie talk - ie to

Alto
(Tenor)

Dan dan dan *etc.*

Piano
(for rehearsal purposes only)

Sud - den - ly a voice said, "Go forth Dad - dy, spread the pic - ture on___ a___
All the way to Can - ton, then to Scran - ton, till he land - ed un - der the Man -

loud and mean, Sud - den - ly a voice said, "Go forth Dad - dy, spread the pic - ture on___ a___
Rock - y Ridge. All the way to Can - ton, then to Scrant - on, till he land - ed un - der the Man -

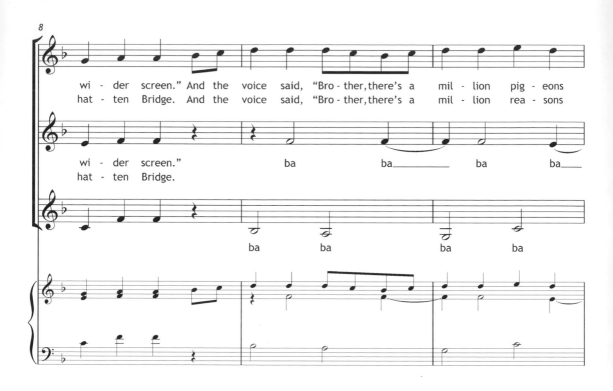

wi - der screen." And the voice said, "Bro - ther, there's a mil - lion pig - eons
hat - ten Bridge. And the voice said, "Bro - ther, there's a mil - lion rea - sons

wi - der screen." ba ba_____ ba ba___
hat - ten Bridge.

ba ba ba ba

rea - dy to be hooked on new re - li - gions. Hit the road, Dad - dy, leave your
why you should be glad in all four sea - sons. Hit the road, Dad - dy, leave you

__ ba ba_____ ba ba_____ ba ba

ba ba ba ba ba ba

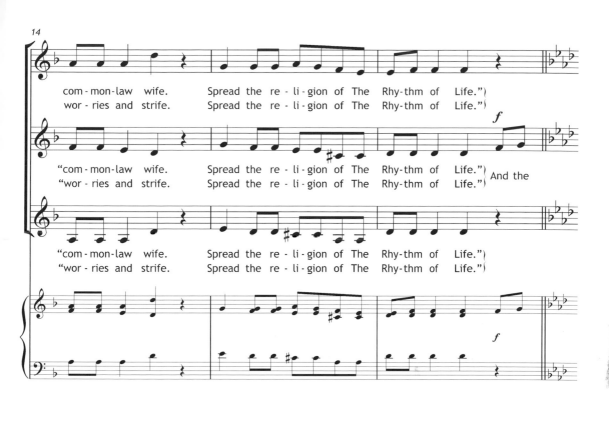

com-mon-law wife. Spread the re-li-gion of The Rhy-thm of Life.")
wor-ries and strife. Spread the re-li-gion of The Rhy-thm of Life.")

"com-mon-law wife. Spread the re-li-gion of The Rhy-thm of Life.")
"wor-ries and strife. Spread the re-li-gion of The Rhy-thm of Life.") And the

"com-mon-law wife. Spread the re-li-gion of The Rhy-thm of Life.")
"wor-ries and strife. Spread the re-li-gion of The Rhy-thm of Life.")

Rhy-thm of Life is a pow-er-ful beat, puts a tin-gle in your fin-gers and a

Dan dan dan etc.

tin - gle in your feet, rhy-thm in your bed - room, rhy-thm in the street, yes, the

To feel the Rhy-thm of Life,

Rhy-thm of Life is a pow-er-ful beat. Yes, the Rhy-thm of Life is a pow-er-ful beat, puts a

to feel the pow-er-ful beat, to feel the

tin-gle in your fin-gers and a tin-gle in your feet, rhy-thm in your bed-room,

1.

tin-gle in your fin-gers, to feel the tin-gle in your feet.

rhy-thm in the street, yes, the Rhy-thm of Life is a pow-er-ful beat.

Oh

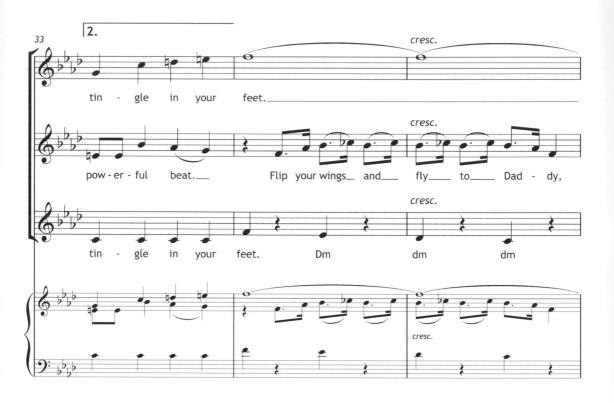

tin - gle in your feet.____

pow - er - ful beat.____ Flip your wings____ and____ fly____ to____ Dad - dy,

tin - gle in your feet. Dm dm dm

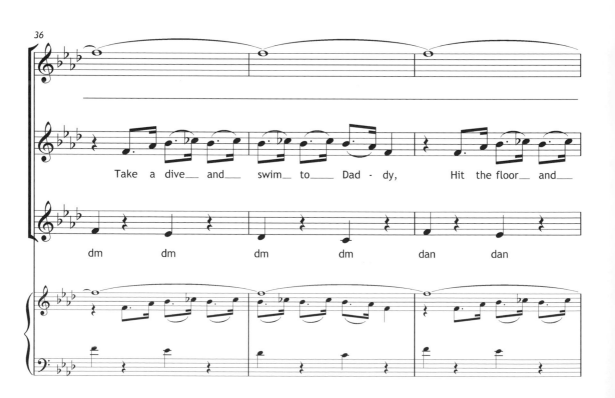

Take a dive____ and____ swim____ to____ Dad - dy, Hit the floor____ and____

dm dm dm dm dan dan

17

One

(from 'A Chorus Line')

WORDS BY EDWARD KLEBAN — MUSIC BY MARVIN HAMLISCH

you know who. One mo-ment in her pre-sence_ and you can for-get the rest,_

you know who. Do do do do do do do do do

you know who. Do do do do do do do do do

—— for the girl is se-cond_ best__ to none, son.

do do do. Da da da da da da da da da da da

do do do. Da da da da da da da da da da da

Pick A Pocket Or Two

(from 'Oliver!')

WORDS & MUSIC BY LIONEL BART

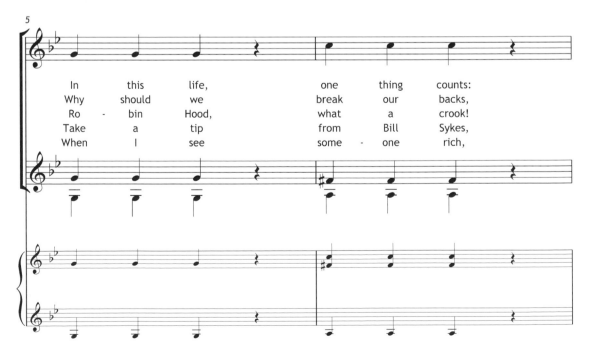

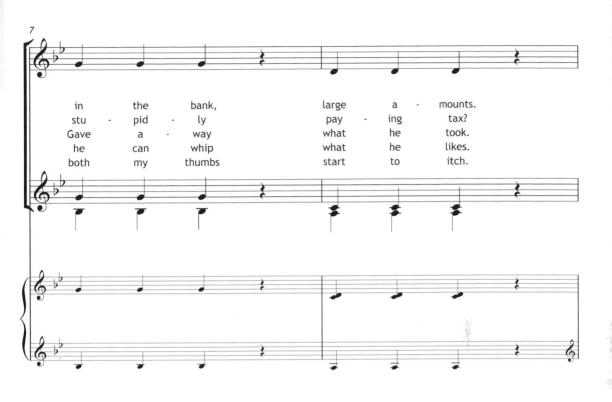

in the bank,   large   a - mounts.
stu - pid - ly   pay - ing   tax?
Gave   a - way   what   he   took.
he   can   whip   what   he   likes.
both   my   thumbs   start   to   itch.

I'm   a - fraid   these   don't   grow   on   trees,   you've
Bet - ter   get   some   un - taxed   in - come,   you'd
Cha - ri - ty's   fine,   sub - scribe   to   mine,   get
I_____   re - call   he   start - ed   small,   he
On - ly   to   find   some   peace   of   mind,   I

Bom   bom   bom   bom

23

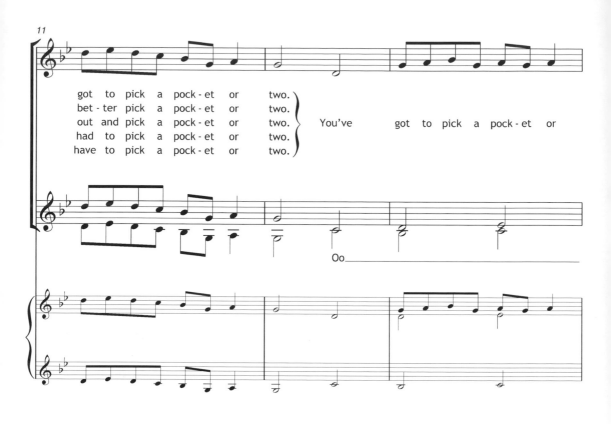

got to pick a pock-et or two.
bet-ter pick a pock-et or two.
out and pick a pock-et or two.
had to pick a pock-et or two.
have to pick a pock-et or two.

You've got to pick a pock-et or

Oo

two, boys. You've got to pick a pock-et or two.

You've got to pick a pock-et or two, or two.

Large a - mounts don't grow on trees, you've
Why should we all break our backs?
Ro - bin Hood was far too good, Get
We can be like old Bill Sykes,
Just to find some peace of mind, we

1-4. **5.** (shout)

got to pick a pock - et or two.
bet - ter pick a pock - et or two.
out and pick a pock - et or two. pa   pa
if we pick a pock - et or two.
have to pick a pock - et or   two.   Hey!

(shout)

Oom   two.   Hey!

Seasons Of Love

(from 'Rent')

WORDS & MUSIC BY JONATHAN LARSON

five hun‑dred twen‑ty five thou‑sand mo‑ments so___ dear.___

five hun‑dred twen‑ty five thou‑sand mo‑ments so___ dear.___ Five hun‑dred,

five hun‑dred twen‑ty five thou‑sand mo‑ments so___ dear.___

Five hun‑dred twen‑ty five thou‑sand six hun‑dred min‑utes. How do you mea‑sure,

five hun‑dred twen‑ty five thou‑sand six hun‑dred min‑utes. How do you mea‑sure,

Five hun‑dred twen‑ty five thou‑sand six hun‑dred min‑utes. How do you mea‑sure,

five hun-dred twen-ty five thou-sand six hun-dred min - utes. How do you mea-sure a

five hun-dred twen-ty five thou-sand six hun-dred min - utes. How do you mea-sure a

five hun-dred twen-ty five thou-sand six hun-dred min - utes. How do you mea-sure a

year in the_ life?_ How a-bout love?_____ How a-bout

year in the_ life?_ love?_____

year in the_ life?_ How a - bout love?_____

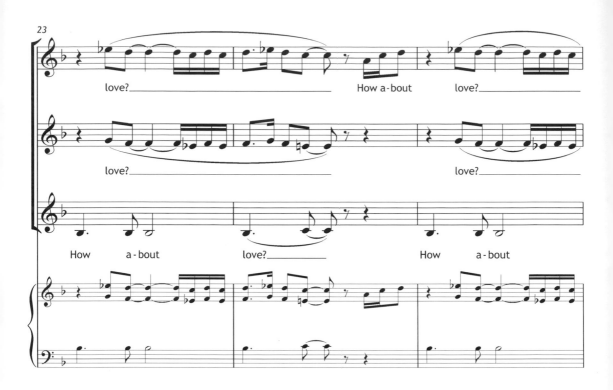

love,_____ sea - sons of

Five hun - dred twen-ty five thou - sand six hun - dred min - utes,

Five hun - dred twen-ty five thou - sand six hun - dred min - utes,

love._____

five hun - dred twen-ty five thou-sand mo-ments so__ dear.   mo-ments so__ dear.

five hun - dred twen-ty five thou-sand mo-ments so__ dear.   mo-ments so__ dear.

Sunrise, Sunset

(from 'Fiddler On The Roof')

WORDS BY SHELDON HARNICK – MUSIC BY JERRY BOCK

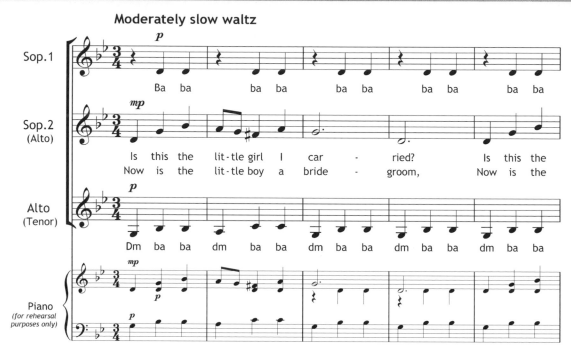

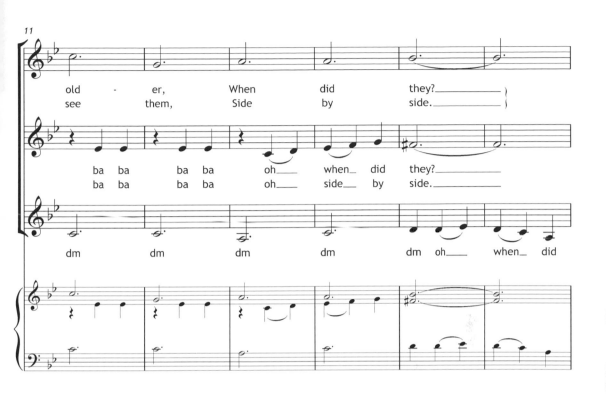

old - er,   When did   they?
see   them,   Side   by   side.

ba   ba   ba   ba   oh___   when___ did   they?
ba   ba   ba   ba   oh___   side___ by   side.

dm   dm   dm   dm   dm   oh___   when___ did

ba   ba   ba   ba   ba   ba   ba   ba   ba   ba

When did she   get to be a   beau   -   ty?   When did he
Place the gold ring a-round her fin   -   ger,   Share the sweet

they? ba ba   dm   ba ba   dm   ba ba   dm   ba ba   dm   ba ba

ba   ba   ba   ba   ba   ba   ba   { Was - n't   it   yes - ter - day when
                                            { Soon the   full   cir - cle will have

grow to   be   so   tall?_____)
wine and break the   glass;_____ } ba   ba   ba   ba   ba   ba   ba   ba

dm   ba   ba   dm   ba   ba   ba   ba   ba   dm   dm

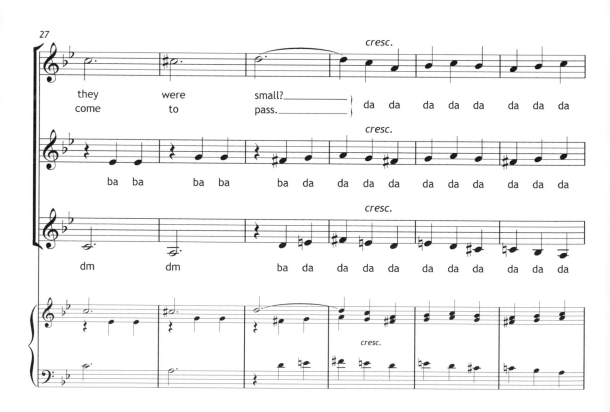

they   were   small?_____)
come   to   pass._____ }   da   da   da   da   da   da   da   da

ba   ba   ba   ba   ba   da   da   da   da   da   da   da   da   da   da

dm   dm   ba   da   da   da   da   da   da   da   da   da   da

cresc.

cresc.

cresc.

cresc.

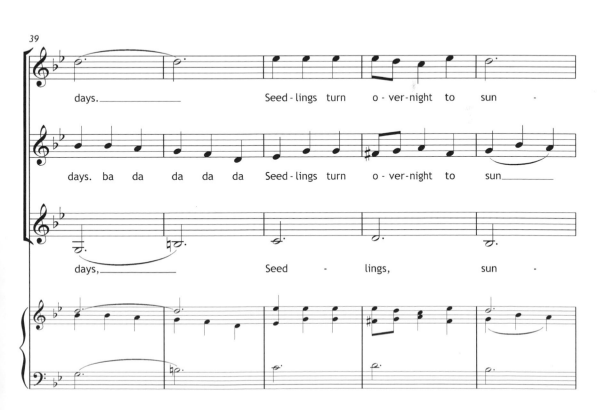

flow'rs, Blos-som-ing ev-en as we gaze._____

flow'rs,_____ Blos-som-ing ev-en as we gaze._____

flow'rs, Blos - som ev - en as____ we

Sun - rise,____ sun - set, Sun - rise,____ sun - set, Swift - ly____ fly the

Sun - rise,____ sun - set, Sun - rise,____ sun - set, Swift - ly____ fly the

gaze, rise, sun - set, fly the

Sit Down, You're Rocking The Boat

(from 'Guy and Dolls')

WORDS & MUSIC BY FRANK LOESSER

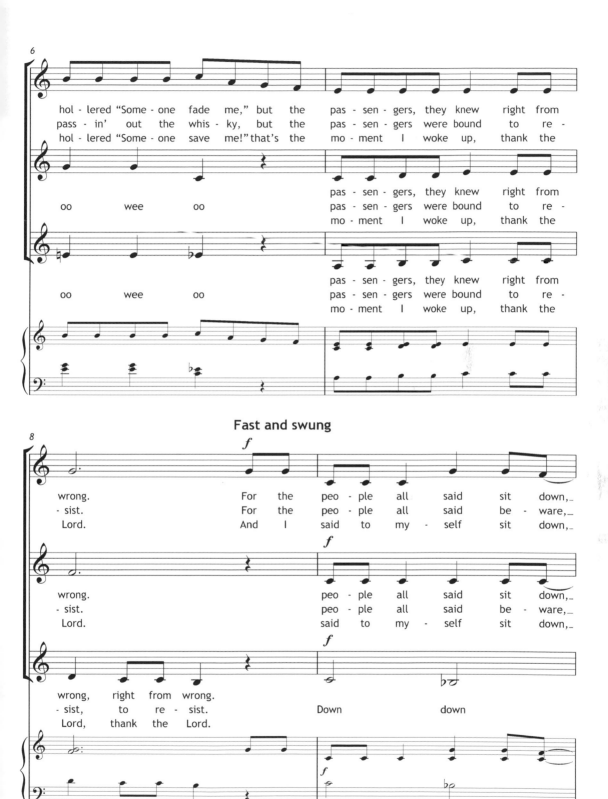

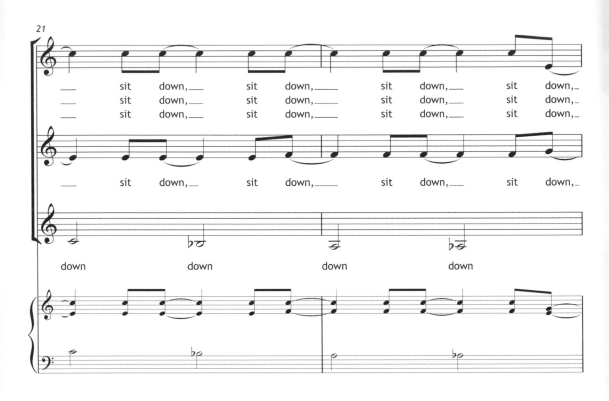

Tomorrow Belongs To Me

(from 'Cabaret')

WORDS BY FRED EBB – MUSIC BY JOHN KANDER

free.   The heart   as   a
sea.   The world   holds   a
bee.   And love   like   a

free.   The heart   as   a
sea.   The world   holds   a
bee.   And love   like   a

fo - rest   runs   free.   The heart   as   a
- sert - ed   the   sea.   The world   holds   a
- bra - ces   the   bee.   And love   like   a

shel - ter   de - fies   the   storm, } to -
pro - mise   that   shines   un -   seen,   } to -
val - ley,   lies   wide   and   deep,   }

shel - ter   de - fies   the   storm, } to -
pro - mise   that   shines   un -   seen,   } to -
val - ley,   lies   wide   and   deep,   }

shel - ter   de - fies   the   storm, } to -
pro - mise   that   shines   un -   seen,   } to -
val - ley,   lies   wide   and   deep,   }

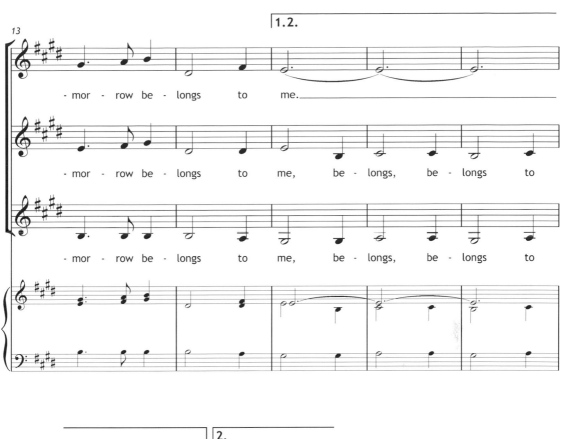

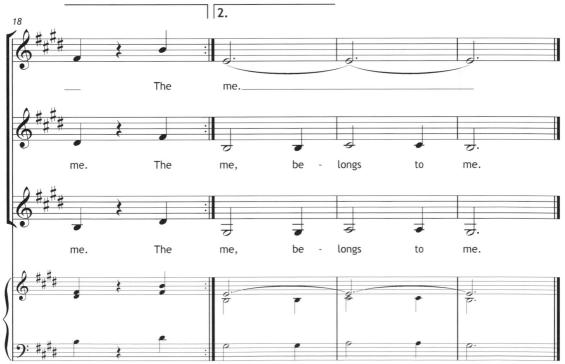

45

Whistle Down The Wind

(from 'Whistle Down The Wind')

MUSIC BY ANDREW LLOYD WEBBER – LYRICS BY JIM STEINMAN

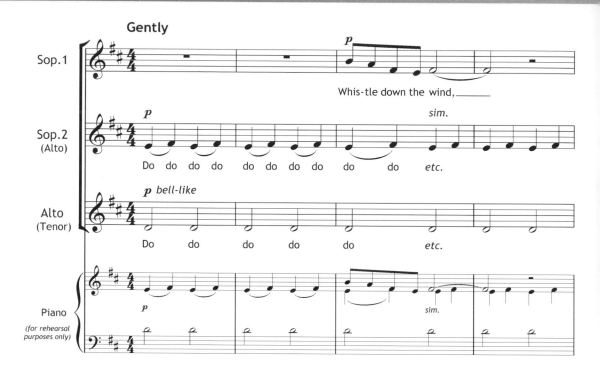

treach-er-ous and sca - ry._____ Howl_ at the stars,_____

whis-per when you're sleep - ing._____ I'll be there to hold you,

I'll be there to stop the chills and all the weep - ing.____ Make it clear and

Make it clear and

Make it clear and

strong so the whole night long____ ev -'ry sig - nal that you send, un -

strong so the whole night long ev -'ry sig - nal that you send, un -

strong so the whole night long ev -'ry sig - nal that you send, un -

-til the ve-ry end, I will not a-ban-don you my pre-cious friend, so

-til the ve-ry end, I will not a-ban-don you my pre-cious friend, so

-til the ve-ry end, I will not a-ban-don you my pre-cious friend, so

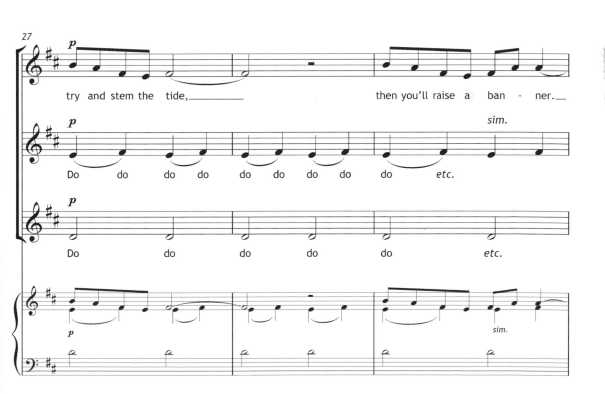

try and stem the tide,_____ then you'll raise a ban - ner._

Do do do do do do do do do *etc.*

Do do do do do *etc.*

Send a flare up in the sky, try to burn a torch and

try to build a bon - fire.___ Do do do do do do do do

Ev -'ry sig - nal that you send un - til the ve -ry end, I'm

51

You'll Never Walk Alone

(from 'Carousel')

WORDS BY OSCAR HAMMERSTEIN II – MUSIC BY RICHARD RODGERS

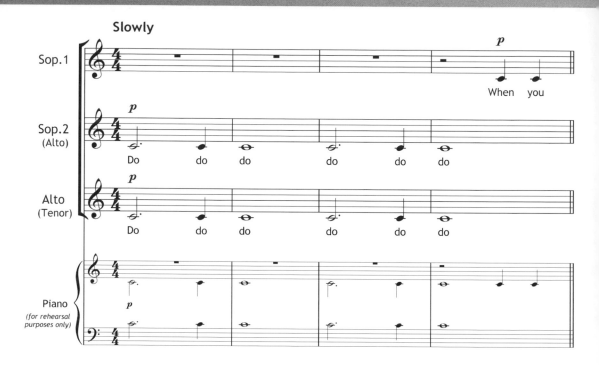

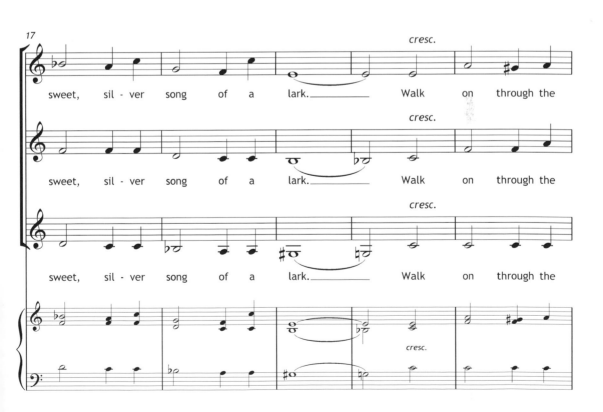

wind, walk on through the rain, though your dreams be tossed and

wind, walk on through the rain, though your dreams be tossed and

wind, walk on through the rain, though your dreams be tossed and

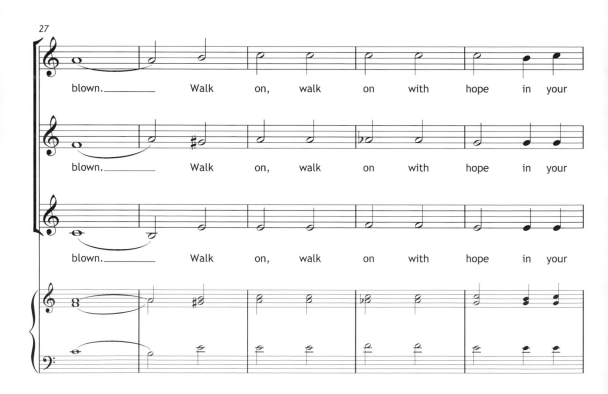

blown.____ Walk on, walk on with hope in your

blown.____ Walk on, walk on with hope in your

blown.____ Walk on, walk on with hope in your

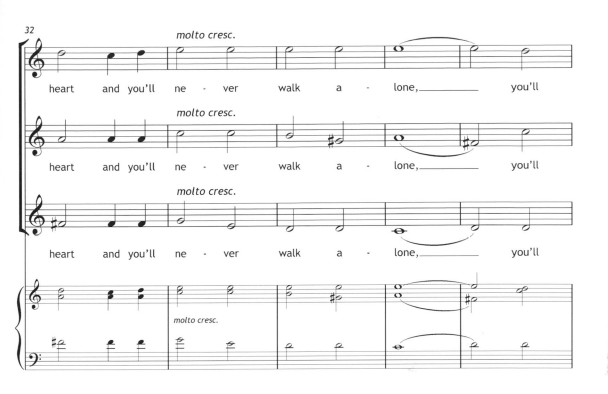

heart and you'll ne - ver walk a - lone,_____ you'll

heart and you'll ne - ver walk a - lone,_____ you'll

heart and you'll ne - ver walk a - lone,_____ you'll

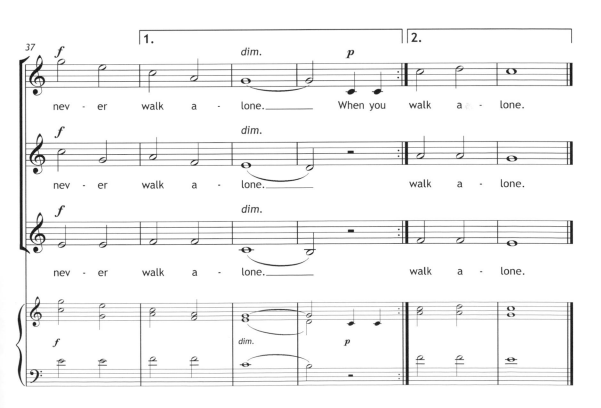

nev - er walk a - lone._____ When you walk a - lone.

nev - er walk a - lone._____ walk a - lone.

nev - er walk a - lone._____ walk a - lone.

Bringing you the words and the music

All the latest music in print... rock & pop plus jazz, blues, country, classical and the best in West End show scores.

- Books to match your favourite CDs.

- Book-and-CD titles with high quality backing tracks for you to play along to. Now you can play guitar or piano with your favourite artist... or simply sing along!

- Audition songbooks with CD backing tracks for both male and female singers for all those with stars in their eyes.

- Can't read music? No problem, you can still play all the hits with our wide range of chord songbooks.

- Check out our range of instrumental tutorial titles, taking you from novice to expert in no time at all!

- Musical show scores include *The Phantom Of The Opera*, *Les Misérables*, *Mamma Mia* and many more hit productions.

- DVD master classes featuring the techniques of top artists.